# At Home in the
# AMERICAN BARN

# At Home in the
# AMERICAN BARN

TEXT BY JAMES B. GARRISON

PHOTOGRAPHY BY

GEOFFREY GROSS AND BRANDT BOLDING

New York · Paris · London · Milan

RIZZOLI INTERNATIONAL PUBLICATIONS, INC.
300 Park Avenue South, New York, NY 10010
www.rizzoliusa.com


ISBN-13: 978-0-8478-4749-5
Library of Congress Control Number: 2015953981


© 2016 Rizzoli International Publications, Inc.
Text (except as noted below) © 2016 James B. Garrison
Photography (unless otherwise noted throughout book)
© 2016 Geoffrey Gross and Brandt Bolding

Distributed to the U.S. Trade by Random House, New York

Endpapers: *Cradle Valley Farm, New Hope, PA (p. 210)*
Page 1: *Barn residence in Washington, CT (p. 108)*
Pages 2–3, 6–7: *Dutch Barn with a Modern Skin, Pine Plains, NY (p. 98)*


Designed by Abigail Sturges Graphic Design


Printed and bound in China

2016 2017 2018 2019 2020 / 10 9 8 7 6 5 4 3 2 1

# Contents

# Introduction

On a farm, the barn is the most important structure. On the frontier, a settler might build a quick temporary residence while he applied his main efforts to constructing the barn. Only after completing this key building would he return to the task of constructing a more permanent dwelling. The barn protected the sources of both his livelihood and his personal needs. Housing livestock and storing feed and grain were all part of the purpose of these buildings. With functionalism a key concern, the buildings adopted basic geometrical shapes to enclose the greatest amount of volume with the most economy. At the same time, the barns employed building and planning traditions brought from the Old World with the abundant resources of the New to create structures that would last for generations.

In the Middle Atlantic colonies, Dutch, English and German settlers were the most important creators of the different barn types. The earliest barns in the New World were built by Dutch settlers from the upper Chesapeake and Delaware Bays up through the Hudson Valley. Their barns are characterized, basically, by a square footprint, with the main wagon entrance centered at the gable end of the moderately pitched roof. The high center space is flanked by lower side aisles in a manner similar to a church. Stalls and storage would be in these lower spaces, with the lofts above for throwing hay and grain for drying and threshing. English barns typically placed the main entrance on the side wall. In some cases, entrances on opposite sides might be on different levels to create separate areas for livestock and crops. Like that of the Dutch barns, the construction was mostly of wood, but the building shape was more rectangular with a more steeply pitched roof.

Many of the German settlers were slightly later arrivals to the middle colonies, with a particular concentration in southeastern Pennsylvania. The abundant fieldstone there led to the creation of the classic stone bank barn. Sometimes, all four walls might be stone, but the gable end walls almost always were, providing strong stabilizing elements for the timber frame in between. On the high side of the site, the centered wagon entrance led to the threshing floor and lofts. The structural ingenuity of the builders often allowed the second floor to overhang the first with a forebay providing a sheltered outdoor space below for the livestock housed on the lower level.

Even some of the earliest barns were truly massive in relation to the houses on the farms. To cope with the structural loads of the building contents as well as wind and gravity, the barns had to be substantially constructed. The virgin hardwood and softwood forests could

*Traditional barns exhibit
very basic building shapes,
as seen in here at Tare Shirt
Farm in Berwick, Maine.*

provide timber of almost any size and shape. There was a considerable art to the way the frames were put together, often without metal fasteners, using traditional methods from the Old World or new techniques derived from the mixing of the builders' different ethnic backgrounds. The elaborate structures could resist high winds, snow loads, and the weight of wagons and livestock. They were always well ventilated to prevent crops from rotting but were stingy with windows, as glass was expensive and taxed. One hundred, two hundred, and even three hundred years after they were built, there was still a lot of utility in these barn buildings and their structural components.

The barns were built to enclose space with a minimum of obstructions, so they can easily become vessels for new uses—in particular, for housing people—but not before some fundamental issues are addressed. After structural stability, the next big issue is providing an envelope for human comfort and habitation. Except for the stone walls in German barns, the buildings had paper-thin skins, meant to give basic protection from the weather and ventilation through gaps in the siding or purpose-built slots. Almost every conversion, even

*Appropriate for a place known as Tare
Shirt, the owner has a special interest in
spinning and weaving. "Tare" refers to a
fine type of linen yarn spun from local flax.*

those where the frame is not moved, strips away the original skin so new insulating wall construction can be added. The thickness of the new walls also provides space for wiring and other infrastructure. Sometimes, exterior siding is used on the inside faces of the new walls and roof to re-create the feeling of the original one-ply siding. Since these walls are typically non–load bearing, there are many opportunities to provide doors and windows without colliding with the timber structure. The approaches here can run from traditional sash units to abstract patterns of glass respond-ing to the interior program or an exterior com-position by the architect.

One part of the original barn structure that was typically not overdesigned was the roof. The slender tapered rafters were fine for the light roofing materials, but modern codes and the need for significant insulation typically require a new structure that might be placed out of sight above the existing roof. In many cases the timber frame becomes a building within a building.

The last great challenges in adaptive re-use of barns are interior conditioning and lighting.

*Preceding pages: A timber frame on full exhibition in a conservatory at Meadow Sweet Farm (p. 114).*

*Facing page: Wood in its many forms from hewn timbers to painted millwork is seen at Old Mill Farm (p. 36).*

*Following pages: Basic barn buildings can be enriched through new construction sensitively added, such as these new windows and doors and the crowning cupola at Bull Frog Pond (p. 58).*

The timber frame that allows for large interior volumes does not create natural opportunities to conceal systems or to create discrete heating and cooling zones. Since many of these rehabilitations involve completely new foundations, there are opportunities for radiant heat in floor slabs, but cooling remains a challenge. At this point, the designers and owners must decide on an aesthetic for these types of interventions, maybe exposed metal ductwork, or something more concealed. Similarly, since old barns relied on natural light, then minimalist electrical lighting, the new interventions might be a mixture of ornamental fixtures and background lighting. The balance again depends on the intended aesthetic. There can be areas of more intense light that focus on particular spaces or objects, and then lighting that brings out the warmth and textures of the interior framing and wall materials. The ability to control the sense of volume with light as well as new construction for subdivided space was a recurring topic with the owners and designers interviewed for this book.

The adaptive re-use of existing buildings is an inherently sustainable undertaking. Barns are a particularly interesting area of this practice since projects might salvage a frame, move it to a new site, and use it as part of a new, larger building, or the barn might be left in place and have minimal interventions. Barn rehabilitations give the owners and designers more freedoms than limitations, chiefly because of the utilitarian origins of the building type. They were buildings that were mixed-use from the start, embodying flexibility due to their open interior plans and simple exterior shapes. The survey of properties in this volume illustrates diverse approaches to a surprisingly common set of programmatic goals for the contemporary owners.

The goals center on interior spaces allowing for personal expression along with exterior treatments that typically emphasize a connection to the particular site. Many owners embarked on their projects as alternatives to more conventional residences, sensing that beginning with a piece of history would set the tone for a dialogue between old and new construction. Happily, these dialogues do not follow the same script. The process can begin with a piece of open land looking for the right kind of building to be placed on it. It might also begin with the artifact, a frame or building looking for a new site. With the building sited, is it an inside-out design process or outside-in? Will the interior program determine how many openings are made in the exterior walls? Are there large areas of glass taking advantage of the post-and-beam framing, or are the windows a more typical residential size to provide for a different scale? Keeping in mind that most barns had very few original windows, the treatment of the exterior envelope is a place where the design can be either free-form or very regular.

Back inside, is the timber frame the major statement in wood, or does wood appear in flooring and sheathing also? Plaster or drywall can show off the hand-hewn textures of the frame and provide a neutral background for the rest of the interior architecture and fur-

*Robust furnishings look very much at home in a timber-framed building, as seen here at Barnesyard (p. 126).*

*Facing page: Painted and stained wood finishes are part of a wide palette available to designers working with timber frames.*

*Following pages: Stone, wood and plaster are all combined in the stairhall of Gronning Barn in Vermont (p. 46) adjacent to the main timber-framed space.*

nishings. Infrastructure can also be in the foreground or background, providing environmental conditioning and lighting. Finally, barns are ideal for collections. Furniture, art, and objects all can find their place, whether they are eclectic pieces or an assemblage focused on a particular aesthetic.

The barns are truly living structures that can adapt continuously to changing needs, whether for agricultural or residential use. The original stone and timber provide basic grounding in space and time. The change of use serves not as a coda but rather as the beginning of a new set of chapters.

# Botsford Hill Farm
## Roxbury, CT

Since its founding over fifty years ago, East Coast Barn Builders has been working with traditional and new technologies to preserve and re-purpose timber buildings for new uses. Ed Cady Sr., now joined by other family members, including his son Ed Jr., have developed innovative techniques for dealing with the challenges of contemporary building codes and four-season habitability. Whether preserved in place or built on new sites, the barn frames and envelopes require significant interventions for their new uses. These begin with foundation systems that actually accommodate two separate buildings, the timber frames and then a new exterior envelope and steel structure to work with the large clear-span spaces below and avoid significant alterations to the antique timbers, which remain exposed in the interior spaces.

The project at Botsford Hill began with a small farmhouse and some existing dairy farm structures set close to the road. In 2001, the Cadys added two salvaged timber frames, creating a new residence substantially larger than the original. The different parts are united on the exterior through the use of reclaimed barn siding that has been prepared to become part of the new envelope by having the nails pulled, the edges trimmed, and a preservative applied. The wood is not resurfaced so as not to obscure the original weathered quality, which provides so much character. Careful installation and access to good source materials allow a feeling of uniformity in siding for these new buildings. The wall and roof cavities behind are well insulated and also pro-vide the space for the new infrastructure required for the residential use.

The second owners of this property brought the Cadys back for another round of renovations that altered the size and shape of some of the windows and changed some interior spaces. John Barman, a designer from New York, collaborated on the interior design to create an interesting dialogue between eclectic Midcentury Modern furnishings and art and the timber frames of the old barn structures. The result is a lively set of spaces where colors and textures interact in a dynamic way that is further enhanced by the new stonework in the fireplaces and construction details in the new stairs and floor levels. Textiles, upholstery, and rugs also make a substantial contribution to the overall effect.

This project is a great example of the flexibility and adaptability of this type of building as it goes through ownership and aesthetic transformations. It also shows how different timber frames can be brought together in a single project to provide a variety of spaces that can then be knit together with careful architectural and interior design interventions. In this case the larger barn frame has the substantial unobstructed multistory volumes to create the great room space. The other structure, with its new silo form, contains smaller-volume spaces with a denser structure of antique framing members. The connections between the building structure and its furnishings also exist between the building and its site. The exterior effect is clearly residential, but the connection to the agrarian past is also very visible.

Facing page: The shapes and
patterns in the furnishings
complement the angular forms
of the surrounding framing.

Within a framed structure,
high and low areas create a
feeling of different rooms
without the addition of walls.

*Facing page: The sliding barn doors with the pair of large roosters are a whimsical room divider.*

*Timbers can be re-assembled in many ways, with the notches for former connections becoming an important part of the texture.*

*Left: Rubble stonework is a natural addition to a timber-framed interior.*

*In this room, the silo form is re-imagined in the cylindrical shape and conical ceiling, with vertical windows for emphasis.*

Timber frames permit a freedom of
window placement that allows for
long and short views.

Facing page: A hidden, supplemental
structure lets exposed framing
be used as a visual element.

Pages 32–35: Botsford Hill Farm enjoys
expansive views over the surrounding
landscape as well as outdoor spaces for leisure.

# Old Mill Farm
## Ghent, NY

Through careful planning and good design, the owners of a small eighteenth-century farmhouse were able to greatly expand their living space by adding an entire historic barn to it without overwhelming the original structure. The position of the house on a gently sloping site overlooking a farm pond helped, but the architect Kate Johns devised a connector link and some additions to the barn that create a coherent arrangement of spaces. The functionality is enhanced by aligning new and old wall openings to provide long views and a sense of orientation in a building with some very different volumes and design motifs.

As a result of sustainable design practices, the larger building uses less energy than the previous residence, relying on geothermal pond loops for heating and cooling and active solar arrays for power generation. Salvaging building materials and sourcing many materials locally were other sustainable practices.

The owners had lived in the smaller house for nearly twenty years when the need for renovations was so great, the radical idea of adding a whole barn was actually not that outlandish. Building technologies had improved to the extent of meeting the energy conservation goals for a year-round residence in an area where there are truly four seasons. The timber framing from an eighteenth-century barn from Washington County in New York was restored by Berkshire Barns from Massachusetts, then re-erected with new energy-efficient walls and structural-integrated panels for the roof. The architect added a sun space overlooking the pond and a clerestory shed dormer for even more natural light in the lofty space. These features along with the double-hung windows help domesticate the scale of the barn and join it to the house. The metal-standing seam roofing and stone foundation walls are other unifying elements.

The connecting link between the house and the added structure is mostly occupied by a stair of Shaker simplicity. The stone house now contains guest bedrooms, a wine cellar and a library. The main volume of the former barn is the common living space for the family, with large masonry chimneys anchoring the kitchen and living room. The light and airy space holds an eclectic array of furniture and decorative objects, from traditional to modern. The wood and masonry appear in rough and highly finished forms to provide different textures and colors as background and foreground in the space. The family bedrooms are on the lower level which is substantially open to grade due to the sloping site.

The owners have found that this new space has allowed them to maintain a more simple and uncluttered lifestyle. A bonus is that it has been accomplished with environmental sustainability as an overarching principal.

The muted color palette and the abundance of natural light create a serene quality in this interior space.

Following pages: The cooking area of the kitchen becomes a significant part of the space as a result of the chimney form that embraces it.

*The pond is an important
landscape feature as well as
being part of a geothermal
heating and cooling system.*

*The fully glazed bay extension
overlooking the pond provides
significant light to the interior and
wide-angle views to the exterior.*

*Old timber posts rest on new granite plinths to create this niche for the bed.*

*Long views from the barn to the house are an important part of the architectural design of the building.*

*Traditional barn features such as this loft ladder were retained to provide smaller-scaled pieces with the heavy timbers.*

Facing page: The owners
have created functional
settings inside the building
for their collection of
architectural artifacts,
art and antique furniture.

# Gronning Barn
## Shaftsbury, VT

When a collection of antiques outgrows a historic house, one response is to create domestic settings in a different structure. In this case, a reconstructed historic barn became the new vessel for the collection. A late-seventeenth-century Dutch barn in the Hudson Valley above Albany was moved about twenty miles east to Shaftsbury, Vermont, where it has become a "Wunderkammer" housing a great collection of early American antiques in a variety of settings made possible by the venerable timber frame of the old barn. The Garret Cornelius Van Ness barn had stood in North Hoosic, New York, for just over 300 years when it was saved from demolition by the present owners, who had the vision to see beyond the inserted ceilings and other construction that obscured the historic material.

The process of finding the building and having it dismantled and re-erected was a living-history experience for the former history teacher and his wife along with their son. Over the course of a year, they thoroughly documented the historic structure, then planned for its re-use, incorporating the best of modern construction materials and assemblies with artifacts from their own collection, including mantelpieces, stairs and woodwork. Stressed skin panels provide insulation, while the windows were made to specially replicate prototypical units found in Holland. The large single sashes pivot on two axes, functioning as hopper windows for moderate ventilation.

The interiors are eclectic, from a formal entry with a black-and white marble floor and an antique stair to the central two-story space that shows off the timbers and joinery. The owners have reimagined an early Dutch house through the use of period details and actual components, with twentieth-century air conditioning and lighting pushed to the background. The lath-and-plaster walls conceal plumbing chases and forced-air ductwork, which weaves its way through the different room-like spaces created within the former barn. The smooth white surfaces of the plaster are also a perfect foil for the different shades and textures of wood, from the floors to paneling and framing members.

The earliest Dutch barns were characterized by broad gables and low eaves. At the time of its completion in 1680, the 50 x 50 foot barn would have been a truly monumental structure. The principal facade of this barn feels firmly planted in the land in its perfect symmetry of new and original wall openings. There is an intriguing dialogue of scales between the large center opening and the regular pattern of single-sash windows. The latter become part of the overall wall texture with the strong shadow lines of the lapped siding. Other modern features like the larger windows or brick chimney occur on secondary facades or at the rear, where they do not compete for attention. Likewise, the garage and antique shop occupy a discretely attached smaller gambrel-roofed structure.

The end result of this thirty-year project is an assemblage of the new and old, various authentic pieces blended with new construction to create a historic home within a historic barn.

In some spaces, the collections
and interior architecture are
the character-defining features.

Facing page: The timber
frame is over 300 years old
and retains a patina that
shows off the furnishings
to fine advantage.

The windows inserted into the
walls give a good sense of the
generous proportions of this
Dutch barn.

Facing page: The "shoulder
spaces" provide room for supporting
functions such as the kitchen and
a second stair to the upper level.

*Roof windows provide natural
light in lieu of dormers, which
would interrupt the uncluttered
roof planes.*

*Some of the upstairs rooms are quite large within the broad-shouldered frame.*

# Dutch Barn Pool House
## Sherman, CT

*The new use required a large number of windows, easily accommodated between framing members.*

*Facing page: The interior effect is light and airy, with the new wood windows blending well with the antique frame.*

*Following pages: The pool has a plaster finish reminiscent of a farm pond.*

Here, on a bucolic wooded site, a Dutch barn frame has been brought in to be the main structure for an indoor pool building. The high center bays and lower side aisles of the barn frame are the perfect form for this use. The wide gable ends provide ample space for new windows, which along with a large cupola provide abundant natural light. Around the pool, light-colored French limestone provides a reflective and durable surface, which has been finished to appear like a natural pond. The new exterior walls and roof structure are well insulated and moisture resistant to work with the dehumidification system that conditions the interior.

Outbuildings, such as this one, are natural extensions of the architecture of the main houses on their respective sites. The mix of the antique and the new in the building materials helps these buildings perform well in their new uses while also being part of the traditional relationship between a residence and its outbuildings.

# Pool House at Bull Frog Pond
## Washington, CT

T he agricultural buildings on a farmstead come in many shapes and sizes to fit the specialized needs of the farm. Smaller buildings might include stables, wagon or tractor barns, and smaller livestock structures. These smaller structures can also be re-purposed and moved to support country houses, which also have requirements for ancillary buildings.

The guesthouse / pool house at Bull Frog Pond complements a new house that replaced a 1950s ranch house that had fallen into disrepair. The new house, designed by Paul Hinkel and constructed by Ed Cady Sr. and Ed Cady Jr., master builders, reflects the characteristics of the turn-of-the-century Colonial Revival dwellings, with its white clapboard siding, heavy cornices and moldings (not featured). As part of the development of the 4.4-acre site, Ed Cady Sr. suggested that a small barn could provide for multiple supporting functions, ranging from a garage to detached guest quarters and a pool house. This building would complete the ensemble while also being consistent with many historical examples of house-and-barn combinations nearby, especially since the barn frame was local.

Set at a right angle to the front of the house, forming part of a forecourt, the small barn has several different themes, depending on which side it is viewed from. Since the site slopes up behind the house, the barn sits on a raised stone foundation that projects forward of the front wall above to provide extra depth in the garage below. The garage doors are rendered as barn doors between the stone piers. Four-square windows with white surrounds punctuate the gray-sided wall above. A white cupola centered on the ridge of the red cedar roof is another domesticating element that ties the barn back to the residence. Another shed lean-to piece on the right-hand side effectively buttresses the construction on the hillside. The gable end that faces the house has two large sliding barn doors at the main level, which open to reveal extra-large double-hung windows with fixed sashes above.

From poolside, the scale is more intimate. The large former wagon entry, now a large pair of doors with a transom, is flanked on either side by a single large window. Karen Davis, the interior designer, brought some of the concepts from the main house into the pool house / guesthouse. The timber frame in the barn is almost understated, given the relatively small size of the building. It divides the white plaster walls into discrete areas occupied by windows or objects that relate to the plain geometry of the frame. The light fixtures, including a large chandelier hung from the cupola, are part of the design that reduces visual clutter in the space. The design concept interprets the original barn for a modern living environment, providing a setting for the American antiques and the red, white and blue color scheme.

*Preceding pages*
*Pages 60–61: The terraced site allows the outbuilding to be multifunctional: a pool house above a garage.*

*Pages 62–63: The poolhouse interiors are less formal than those for the house, built around a color palette of red, white, and blue.*

*Left: The interior details make use of rough-sawn wood and utilitarian hardware.*

*Bottom left: The interior stair leads from the lower-level garage to the upstairs poolhouse.*

*Right: The pool house furnishings are scaled to relate to the more intimate volume of the space.*

*Following pages*
*Pages 66–67: In the main house, the timbers are a design element rather than part of the building structure.*

*Page 68: New and old materials create an interesting dialogue on the exterior.*

*Page 69: The handwrought quality of the chandelier complements the wood framing and planking of the roof structure.*

# Minglewood
## Roxbury, CT

The Minglewood barn home is an assemblage of antique timber frames and materials knit together with new construction to form the present residence. At first, the design used only one main barn frame, with all bedrooms on the second floor. Late in the process, having all of the main living spaces on one level increased in priority, so the master suite was moved down a floor. A new wing was required for this change. A great side effect on the main barn was that it gained a sun-filled double-height great room. Then a mudroom, breezeway, and garage wing were added off the kitchen, still preserving the main barn frame. In this way, a compact house design grew into something much larger. This extra volume could have been overwhelming but instead offered options for a variety of living spaces and decorating opportunities.

The owners had been searching for property for a while, looking for something that had an antique quality, but big spaces and the possibility of modern touches. Their Realtor suggested the idea of a barn conversion. After they purchased the vacant land, the first challenge was having the town extend the road for vehicular and utility access. Bringing power a long distance off the main road was a particular challenge because the lines had to be buried to respect a landing-and-takeoff easement for a defunct airstrip adjacent to the property, and then once on the property, the lines were also buried so they wouldn't be seen.

Ed Cady, founder of East Coast Barn Builders worked with architect Paul Hinkel of Bristol, Connecticut, to fashion the 11,000-square-foot residence from multiple sources of materials. The main barn frame was unusual in that it allowed two full living levels under the eave line and loft space above. With some judicious removals of the second-floor framing, they created a variety of interior volumes and opportunities for large window openings. Putting the antique frame back together was a five-month project for a crew of six or seven, and the result was a building within a building, since there is unseen structure that carries the load of the slate roof and provides space for insulating walls.

Much of the other building material either was local or had a connection to agricultural buildings. The stone for the massive chimneys came from nearby and relates well to the slate in the roofs. The siding is from tobacco barns and possesses a weathered feeling that is part of the dialogue between the old and new construction in the building. The new structure allowed a great deal of freedom in placing windows, which enabled a light and airy feeling inside the large building. At night, a combination of low-voltage and conventional light fixtures provide options. Ken Daniel consulted on the lighting, including the custom interior lantern made in Texas. The interior spaces manage the difficult balance of being very open, yet also cozy.

The project began as a weekend home but became a full-time residence after six years. The design, with all of the major living spaces on one level, still worked well. The second floor of the large center section has guest suites, loft space, and a bridge to a second level over the master suite. The master bath is in another small connected building with a monitor skylight providing a continuous trough of light for the different spaces within that footprint.

*Preceding pages: The doors and windows represent a different scale from the frame; they float in plain plaster wall surfaces.*

*Left: Views from the balcony level give a sense of the large interior volume.*

*Facing page: The lightness of the wood chairs is a surpising contrast to the heavy timbers.*

*Following pages
Pages 76–77: Bridges and open balconies become natural extensions of the main frame and provide a more domestic scale to the interior volume.*

*Pages 78–79: Several barn frames were used to complete the ensemble of buildings on the site.*

Facing page: The site
contained several red barns,
the smallest of which was
turned into a residence.

# Beyond the Red Barn
## Millbrook, NY

This classic red barn complex in Dutchess County, New York, has evolved over the past 200 years through different agricultural and non-agricultural uses. The land was part of the "Nine Partners Patent," dating from the end of the seventeenth century, then moving into the ownership of several generations of farmers of German descent. After the farm passed from that series of owners, it became a dairy operation with the group of buildings that survives to this day. The smallest structure, once a manger and storage facility, was built from materials most likely taken from the older barns on the property. The dairy operation continued to 1960, when the farm was sold again.

In the late 1980s the small barn was converted to a painting studio with the addition of skylights, board-and-batten siding, and new windows. At that time, the entire interior was also painted white as a neutral backdrop for the studio. In order to make the space somewhat self-sufficient, a sleeping loft, small kitchen and bathroom were also added.

The present owners redesigned the interior in 2000 to reflect their tastes and interests and provide a more residential ambience as a weekend getaway. The interiors now incorporate fabrics from her textile designs and furniture he built to complement the antiques and other pieces from their collection. The maple fall-front desk by the bed is one of the pieces he built.

The three-building ensemble forms a balanced composition at the edge of a meadow with a small orchard that helps define a spatial boundary for the group. The converted studio does not proclaim its residential use loudly, especially from the approach. As a container for new and old objects, it is very successful in the way the white paint mutes the different textures of the construction, providing just enough counterpoint for the new furnishings and fabrics, which offer hints of color and softness. Like many re-purposed barn interiors this one has layers of geometry and meaning from the old hewn timbers, the sawn vertical studs, and the horizontal board interior siding, which provide the point of departure for the new use.

*Preceding pages
Pages 82–83: The
whitewashed wood
neutralizes the background
to emphasize the textiles
and furnishings.*

*Pages 84–85: The
abundant natural light
highlights the softness of the
furnishings and fabrics.*

*Left: The mixture of sawn
and natural framing is a
visual link back to the
building's utilitarian
origin.*

*Facing page: The fall-front
desk was designed and built
by the owner.*

*Following pages: The group
of buildings in a pasture
overlooks a small brook in a
truly rustic setting.*

*Facing page: The open kitchen with its pizza oven was a defining feature of the interior design. Photograph by Katie Morning.*

# Where Bauhaus Meets Barn

## Roxbury, CT

It has been a common theme that many people undertaking barn conversions are simply looking for more space. Whether one is moving from a confining urban location or a small country house, a barn offers all kinds of possibilities and spaces. This 220-foot-long former dairy barn turned residence is toward the extreme end of the spectrum. The owners, a photographer and filmmaker and his family, were living in an eighteenth-century house in Fairfield County, but his new experimental pursuits required more space and a different setting for inspiration. It was time for an aesthetic and physical change. An empty wood-and-masonry barn built in 1962 was the answer. Not a traditional barn, it represented the modern, twentieth-century approach to dairy farming. There was one level for the animals, with a concrete floor and 90 stalls with abundant light and air from the numerous square windows punctuating the long, low walls below the soaring roof. The building offered not only opportunities for his interests but space for family and friends to gather around a new hearth and kitchen area. The planning process was very much a shared task.

In order to maximize the volume under the cathedral-like loft, the concrete floor had to be removed and lowered to create enough headroom below the floor level of the loft studio. The new construction enabled the new residential heating and plumbing systems to be incorporated along with a spectacular great room. This is where Bauhaus meets barn, with the steel factory sash creating a transparent corner topped by a shallow barrel vault. Inside, the grids of the window mullions and the tile floor contrast with the free-form sculpted shape of the fireplace and conversation area.

Up a short flight of steps is the open kitchen, where a pizza oven shares the chimney with the fireplace below. From there one enters the body of the former dairy space, where the linear arrangement of stalls has given way to an undulating center gallery with the bedrooms to either side. The final curving element is a stair to the 5,000-square-foot studio above with an additional bedroom suite.

This loft space shows how the engineering and manufacturing improvements of the twentieth century created entirely different barn interiors from the heavy timber frames of the preceding era. The light, curved framing members create a strong, very elegant unobstructed space, very different from the gang nail trusses now employed for this type of construction or the pegged rafters of eighteenth- and nineteenth-century barns. This type of dairy barn represents a high point in the specialized construction that respected the history of the building type while introducing the most up-to-date building and farming technology, from the milking hall to the enameled steel Harvestore silo still attached to the building.

The conversion took nearly eighteen months to complete and served the owners for fourteen years before other film industry commitments caused them to move to the West Coast. The unique interiors always felt cozy for them whether with just a few guests or with several hundred. The great room became a theater with nature the stage.

The great room extension borrows from the original roof form but is wholly transparent, in contrast to the rest of the former dairy barn.

*Following pages*
*Pages 94–95: A conversation area with a kiva-type fireplace is a group of organic forms in a Bauhaus-inspired space. Photograph by Katie Morning.*

*Pages 96–97: The fully glazed great room has views over the valley in two directions, with polished light flooring amplifying the natural light.*

Facing page: The horizontal
board siding with monolithic
glazing is a distinctly
modernist expression of a non-
load-bearing building skin.

# Dutch Barn
# with a Modern Skin
## Pine Plains, NY

This barn makes a strong statement about the relationship between the different technologies of the timber frame inside and the outside skin. The abstract placement of different window shapes, rendered as simple cutouts in a thin membrane, is a strong contrast to the rational forms of the antique timber frame. The interface between these two systems is a tubular steel space frame, which, in a sense, is the timber frame rendered again in a contemporary material. The thin steel frame repeats the rectilinear and diagonal forms of the timber for visual as well as structural reinforcement.

The path to this conversation of materials and forms was long and deliberate. The apparent contradictions between low-tech folk art forms and modern expressions and objects required a deft touch from the owners and the design and construction teams. Each team member brought special sensibilities. Scott Cohen from Harvard's Graduate School of Design brought the rich tradition of the post-war modernists, while Jack Sobon's expertise with timber-frame restoration ensured that this precious relic maintained its integrity inside its new skin. The owners found a 165-acre parcel near the Connecticut border that provided a site with expansive views over the rolling hills. Their collection of objects ranging from a traditional French farm table and Dutch-inspired antique kass (armoire) to Bertoia and Le Corbusier chairs lives comfortably in the space, where the timber frame is both a foreground and background element.

The residence contains four bedrooms and four baths located on mezzanines surrounding the large center volume, except on the west side where the building opens up to the long views and afternoon light. The frame itself is larger than the typical square-footprint barn from the period, measuring 50-by-60 feet. This extra plan area made a big difference in allowing for features like an "indoor/outdoor" common space separating the different zones within the building. The polished concrete main floor forms a neutral background, like the concrete fireplace mass with its stainless steel stovepipe. Metal also finds its way in through the thin steel railings and theatrical pipe grid lighting supports. Birch plywood partitions complement the heavy timber and, like the fireplace, become sculptural elements in the space.

This weekend retreat is yet another take on the adaptive re-use of barn frames in that it uses an unabashed modern skin as a wrap, or, as the designer says, "the transported and re-erected Dutch barn frame is contained in this house like a guitar in its case." Even though the exterior has an unconventional arrangement of windows, the Dutch barn heritage is clear in the simple overall geometry and proportions of the roof shape to the base. The narrow horizontal siding imparts a more neutral texture than the more typical wide vertical boards. This structure shares the site with some additional smaller barns and agricultural structures serving, as a guesthouse and various storage functions.

*Preceding pages: The timber frame reads as an curious artifact within concrete, steel and the structural panel building shell.*

*Left: In some views, the timbers become the background to the objects and artwork.*

*Right: Theatrical pipe grid and steel conduit link the lighting to the timber frame.*

*Following pages*
*Pages 104–05: The raw concrete fireplace is a different "natural" texture from the polished floor and hewn timbers.*

*Pages 106–07: The Dutch barn form is still apparent behind the abstraction of the window openings in the thin membrane skin.*

*Facing page: The interior
architecture is a backdrop
to the owner's furnishings.*

# The Third Time's the Charm
## Washington, CT

Three is the charm for architect Russell Groves in the design of a re-purposed barn residence in Connecticut, his third project for the same clients for whom he designed a house and office in New York. In many ways this was a different challenge from their Brooklyn Heights town house and the owner's office in Manhattan, though some of the same principles were employed, such as the creative tension between the old and new, and the provision of spaces for work and play. Both residences had to work for family life with children as well as more serious activities. They also each began with a nineteenth-century structure. The mid-nineteenth-century barn came from Canada and had been re-erected and fit out by a previous owner, who also had the pool house on the grounds built in a sympathetic style.

Groves provided a big refresh to the buildings, updating the technology as well while incorporating some thoughtful details to provide a better setting for the owners' varied furnishings, which tend to objects spanning the entire twentieth century. The timber frame and natural wood floors provide a unifying background for all of the new objects, which bring different colors and textures to the space. In the process, the building also became more child-friendly through changes to the stair and balcony railings as well as more casual furniture. The architect also designed some of the furniture, including the four-poster bed in the master suite, and commissioned other pieces to make a more coherent statement about new things in a traditional container.

Lighting was also a very important part of the design, from Noguchi floor lamps to custom chandeliers. The architect characterizes the effect as "warm modernism." In the kitchen, a zinc-lined rustic sink and marble countertops go with sleek modern appliances to continue the dialogue between old and new. Vintage movie posters and contemporary abstract art provide more contrasts that expand the breadth of the overall design.

Arrayed in a line across a gently sloping site, the barn and pool house present an organized arrangement and repetition of forms, materials and colors. The large areas of windows domesticate the "red barn," along with landscaping around the buildings and pool.

In working with "found objects," the job of the designer is to write a new chapter for new owners. Russell Groves has used furniture and a light touch inside to close the gap between the antique and the contemporary, much the way he used landscape elements outside to unify the composition of the site.

*Different expressions in wood.*

*Right: Soft forms and colors promote a feeling of comfort and repose.*

*Following pages: The pool house and barn residence are a natural pairing of details and overall geometries.*

Facing page: The main entry
is through a silo form whose
windows give a watchtower effect.

# Meadow Sweet Farm
## Bridgewater, CT

There are still many large farms in upper Litchfield County, Connecticut. The buildings on the farms have changed along with farming methods, becoming larger, with new sections for new uses. At Meadow Sweet Farm, the original farm buildings remain on the site, but on the hill beyond, deep into the property, there is another complex of buildings forming the new main residence. The 15,000-square-foot home, incorporating three different barn frames, does not look out of scale on the landscape; nor do the parts from different sources betray different origins.

East Coast Barn Builders has created a unified building from the many parts, using reclaimed siding and various groupings of windows, dormers and chimneys to compose the exterior facades. In the entrance court, a silo form becomes a hinge point between the largest barn section and a projecting wing. The lower, broader forms of the other wings hint at the interior uses through groupings of windows looking out into the surrounding meadows or smaller individual units in the courtyard and service wing. A projecting conservatory uses large, undivided insulating glass units between the hewn timbers of the wall and roof structure, creating an effect of no walls or roof when looking out from the inside.

Inside, the different frames allow for different types of interior space: large double-height volumes, connecting links with overlooks, or more intimate spaces. The main entrance is through the new silo form, where an open-riser curved stair lets the light shine through into the connecting hall that leads to the great room on one side and the kitchen on the other. The massive stone chimney is the principal device that divides the space in the great room, as the timbers and diagonal braces wrap around it. The kitchen features timber trusses and a large bay window.

The main house and its outbuildings are just one part of the overall site plan for the property. Most of the land remains open pasture, with stands of trees following old property and field boundaries. There is a soft transition from meadow to lawn, and small groups of trees and pieces of site-specific sculpture give scale to the setting and provide measuring points for the panoramic views. The two entrance drives converge to a point where the residence comes slowly into view on the brow of the hill, not revealing its particular architectural features until the visitor is close, and then one must enter the residence to fully appreciate how traditional timber barn frames have become the signature feature of a truly gracious country home.

*Preceding pages: The main stair spirals up through the silo form.*

*Left: Stone is an anchoring element for the timber frames.*

*Right: Long views show the curves, diagonals and rectilinear geometries of the wood in the building.*

*Following pages: The kitchen receives light from skylights, French doors and a large bay.*

A whimsical object relates to
the various forms of wood in
the structure and
furnishings.

Right: Another well-lit
space is this second floor
connecting balcony.

Following pages: The naked
frame encloses a timber-
framed conservatory.

# Barnesyard
## Sergeantsville, NJ

The purchase of a post–Civil War barn in 1994 inspired not only a place to live, but a way of life as well. It had been split off from the parcel containing the original house and partially renovated. It also came with something special—a small donkey named Ernest and a large draft horse named Chester. The new owners adopted these animals and later many others, establishing the farm as a place for homeless animals. Author Laura Barnes made the donkey the subject of a series of illustrated children's books featuring Ernest and his barnyard friends.

While looking after Ernest and his friends, the owners lived in the barn for nine years before undertaking the present restoration project, which has resulted in something both traditional and uniquely contemporary. The completed building houses animals below and people above, an arrangement found on traditional farms in Europe and other parts of the word. It reflects both an economy of construction and the symbiotic relationship between farmers and their livestock. In colder months the natural body heat from large animals helps warm the space above, and in the summer, the upper floors are a buffer from the sun for the animals below. One could think that these shared quarters might be too close for contemporary living, but Laura Barnes explains that the new construction has allowed the degree of closeness to be regulated through insulation and space conditioning. Opportunities remain for contact, such as trap doors where hay was previously dropped into the stalls below.

The present building is an engaging synthesis of materials also. Wood is a very important material here, from the well-worn floorboards to the ladders and stairs added to the interior. A large new outdoor deck allows the master suite to become part of the pasture, while a new wood portico employs a special timber to create a strong entrance statement. The rhythm of the large and small windows creates an expectation of unique spaces within, which is fulfilled by the varied volumes and extraordinary flea-market finds that complement the furnishings inside. A former workbench with its vise still attached now functions as a side table. The decorative aspects of antique farm implements are especially appropriate to the environment. Some of the larger pieces simply wouldn't fit in a typical interior space.

Keeping part of the barn true to its original purpose was important in establishing a mood for the whole property. Gardens, pastures, wood and stone are all part of the spirit of the place. Neither the building nor the site has been overly domesticated. The natural surroundings and presence of animals in the building bring a sense of warmth and serenity—pure magic.

Preceding pages: The trussed structural bent provides a clear span carrier for the upper floor level.

Left: The exposed sprayed-in ceiling insulation also helps to soften the acoustics.

Facing page: The owners' collection of large and small farm implements and other objects is at home in the varied spaces of the building.

Following pages: Objects collected over time from flea markets have been curated to relate to the different types of space in the residence.

*Even the smaller spaces benefit from the variety of found objects.*

# Traditional Meets Modern
## New Hope, PA

The story of this barn conversion is a series of unlikely and unforeseen events, not unlike the stories of others seeking a different type of residential experience. The owners had lived in a small farmhouse and then a contemporary minimalist dwelling by Hugh Newell Jacobsen, known for his pavilion-like buildings based on simple geometrical shapes. They came to this property in Bucks County, Pennsylvania, intending to renovate the farmhouse rather than the barn. When the house project appeared to be more difficult than expected, they made the larger leap to the barn renovation. The derelict building, home to generations of bats, spoke to the clients because of the spatial opportunities it offered.

The barn project combined aspects of their former residences—the light and airy feeling of the Jacobsen residence and the warm and inviting atmosphere of the farmhouse. Mixing old and new materials was one strategy to synthesize the different qualities of their previous residences. The end result is a compelling conversation between materials, interior spaces and construction methods from different eras. Traditional forms and several periods of Modernism are reflected in the architecture and furnishings of the new residence. The original barn volume has most of the living spaces, but it is supplemented by a connection through a rebuilt silo to a new bedroom wing.

The original timbers become an abstracted three-dimensional space frame with the bents arranged in the traditional vertical bays and also horizontally around a new chimney mass and stabilizing elements for the largely glazed gable end wall. The diagonal bracing on two planes creates this strong geometrical abstraction, which adds a dimension to a typical barn frame. Instead of pegs, mortises and tenons, the timber frame joints are emphasized with reinforcing blocks and exposed hardware. On a smaller scale, a glass and stainless steel railing system uses the same interplay between structural members and connectors to produce a construction diagram. Bright steel spiral ductwork continues the theme of metal. Wide-plank floors and an exposed wood roof deck bring that material back into the conversation between elements.

This barn project accentuates the qualities of traditional architecture that the early modernists found so compelling—simple geometrical forms, open plans, and rational structure. The purposeful alterations to the structure, the interior volume, and the building skin take this project to the opposite end of the spectrum from conversions that emphasize the antiquarian qualities of barns. The shape of the building is unmistakably traditional, but the forebay becomes more like a greenhouse with its fully glazed corner. At night, the gable end reveals the exceptional transparency and unconventional diagonal bracing added to the frame.

The furnishings also complement the modernist rather than traditional take on the barn form by representing a range of eras and aesthetics from the Barcelona chairs and spiral stair of the International Style through Midcentury modern to late modern with the glass and stainless railing systems and recent furniture. The lighting adds a whole other layer of whimsy to spaces with varied types of fixed and pendant fixtures adding different scales and effects.

One of the goals of the project was to make interesting spaces. Guests would feel a sense of excitement by the juxtapositions of materials and objects, but also see the comfortable aspect. Here, the barn was a great point of departure, but its history and basic qualities were never lost or forgotten.

*Preceding pages: The interior timber frame is a three-dimensional space frame with bracing on horizontal and vertical planes.*

*Steel, glass and concrete supplement the original wood frame.*

*Facing page: Modern technology is in full view, in the structural frame, HVAC or electrical fixtures, and conduit.*

Preceding pages: The architectural design emphasizes connections between different materials and their surface textures.

Outside of the main volume, the interior design is minimalist.

Right: The wide range and juxtaposition of architectural elements and furnishings is meant to be provocative.

Following pages: At night, the large window areas illuminate the elaborate geometry of the building frame.

# Westwind Orchard
## Accord, NY

Sustainability can have many definitions in the contemporary world. The owners of Westwind have embraced the ethic on many levels, from land and building stewardship to a lifestyle with deep roots in their cultural heritage. The story began many years ago when the owners found a property that spoke to them. On one level, the old orchard was reminiscent of the rural landscapes in Italy, where the current owners had been born, but then other parallels with the previous owner emerged in how his interests were enriched by a life in the country.

After living in the eighteenth-century farmhouse on the property for ten years and becoming self-taught farmers, they were ready to renovate some of the rest of the existing farm buildings to support a growing business in produce from the 33-acre farm. The timber barn on site was disassembled, then re-erected in a broad meadow, where it became the place where jams, vinegars, produce, and honey from the farm could be prepared for sale. The building retains the functionality of a barn in its large spaces and spare finishes while providing a place for the more eclectic furnishings the owners have gathered or made over the years. From the Moroccan rug to the large table, the furnishings contribute to the strong sense of place in the building. The luxury in this building is the space itself and its rawness. Some of the strong texture comes from the use of mushroom wood, planks reclaimed from old mushroom farms. Its exposure to the mushroom-growing process leaves it with a unique raised grain and color.

The strength of the present design comes from the simplicity of the original building and how the adaptation has complemented, rather than competed with, the original fabric. The exterior is the most elemental form of a plain gabled rectangular box where the studied symmetries and asymmetries of new and old openings create just the right amount of tension. The gable ends are different from each other and from the two other facades, where the large sliding doors on opposing sides allow the meadow to flow through the building, uninterrupted by the smooth concrete floor. The colors and textures of the standing-seam roof and vertical siding are also complementary, with the small metal stovepipe barely catching attention.

The re-use of buildings has a visible gesture to sustainability like organic farming. Creating a place that speaks to a sustainable lifestyle is more subtle. The owners are not full-time farmers, so the country is only a part of their life, but it sustains their creativity in other professions. Nature and the balance of nature, which are so much a part of organic farming, constant inspirations. There is always a surprise, since while the seasons come and go, other things might not be so constant. People are really affected by the place, so much so that one person asked permission to make his wedding proposal there. The future has more things in store for Westwind, from active solar-power generation to more experiences for the owners and visitors.

*There is a purity about the
harmony between the
architecture and the interior
design that is in keeping with
the organic produce of the farm.*

Left: Simplicity rules in both the building and the furnishings.

Nature is never very far away at Westwind Orchard.

Above left: The simple farmhouse kitchen is part of the production line from field to table.

Below left: In their closed position, the sliding barn doors add a vertical accent to the interior wall surfaces.

Facing page: Each facade of the building possesses its own symmetry, which reinforces the object quality of the building in the meadow.

154

*Facing page: The location
for the barn deliberately sets
off lawn areas in the center
against wilder landscaping
at the edges of the site.*

# Middleton-Waln Barn
## Watermill, NY

The New Jersey Barn Company, founded by Alex Greenwood and Elric Endersby in 1977, had rescued many middle Atlantic timber barns by 1992 when the Middleton-Waln barn in North Crosswicks, New Jersey, was relocated to the South Fork of Long Island to serve as an inexpensive weekend retreat. In making the journey, it adopted some of the forms of the local Long Island vernacular in the cedar shingle siding and white painted double- and single-sash windows. With a footprint of only 26-by-36 feet it is a modestly sized English barn, yet it contains some interesting framing details in the four bents that form the three-bay structure. The onetime stall area has denser framing and a loft that forms a modest mezzanine overlooking the center bay, whose large wagon opening, adapted with glass sliding doors, sidelights and transoms really light up the interior space. The other edge of that volume is defined by a great brick fireplace mass relating to an old forge with twin metal stovepipes breaking through the roof plane on either side of the ridge.

The original bank barn had a cramped lower level, which gained headroom when the timber frame was placed on a new concrete foundation on a site that offered a bit more slope. The lower level contains two bedrooms and storage areas.

The foundation was also elongated to accommodate an additional bay, denoted by the triple window on the principal facade. This addition can be separated from the rest of the residence by sliding doors to the library space on the first floor and the master suite on the second.

This building demonstrates many of the features that make barn conversions compelling works of architecture. The historic timber frame has been preserved with minimal changes so it still demonstrates the essential qualities of its handmade construction. The simple geometry of the barn shape has been extruded and placed on a higher base to provide more living space, again without losing the essential qualities of the building. Subtle cues of more windows, and different rhythms of openings, distinguish the additions without being dissonant. Finally, the exterior skin, replaced to provide four-season habitability, has adopted the materials of the new setting without a clash of scales.

This building was not meant to become a Long Island beach house, but instead it relates to the more utilitarian local heritage of agriculture and light industry. It does this in a very private setting where the manicured lawns meet the wild meadows and a New Jersey barn becomes a comfortable New York residence.

The brick fireplace and double
stack is a room divider in the
large open space.

Facing page: The large
openings in the center of each
long exterior wall create a
strong cross axis of light.

The interior design of the rooms added in the barn extension continues the informal rustic aesthetic.

Right: Some of the interior details and furnishings preserve the agricultural origins of the building.

Following pages: The extension of the original symmetrical English barn form allowed for more living space and some smaller rooms, as evidenced by the number of windows on the right-hand side.

# A Celebration of Wood and Universal Space

## Old Chatham, NY

This barn residence in Old Chatham, New York, represents a response to the opportunities presented in a partially completed transformation. From her 1920s stone house in suburban Philadelphia, the owner came to a building that had been renovated as a party barn and office. From a conventional Colonial Revival setting defined by plaster walls and wood moldings, she developed a structure that celebrates wood in all of its forms and a modernist "universal space." This residence is primarily about living in one room while the other functional requirements are consigned to smaller supporting structures attached to the main volume.

The ten-year project added a kitchen in a small structure to the left of the main entrance and bedrooms in another pavilion on the other side. Inside and out, the main theme is wood showing its natural colors and textures. Sometimes it is hand-hewn structural members, other times round logs or furniture joinery for new elements. There are also some salvaged domestic pieces like a colonial-era mantel, doors and paneling. The basic frame and form are in character with a Dutch barn from, the square footprint and shallow roof pitch to the way the main structural bents are assembled. The open frame allowed for mezzanine lofts for a library, as well as more intimate spaces off the main volume. The lofts and new stairs are characterized by construction detailing that demonstrates the versatility of wood as a building material and the master builders who fashion it into useful structures.

Rather than sawn floor joists or structural planks, the loft floor construction employs an underlying structure of small logs laid side by side. Both the underside and end conditions provide visual interest and varied textures. The stairs take a different approach, with simple stringers and open risers pegged together with wedges, like the original timber frame.

The interior and exterior siding also allows the character of the wood to show, with knotholes and irregular edges contrasting with the long horizontal lines of each course of planking. One of the more eye-catching details is the intersection of one of the ancillary structures with the main barn. The architect has allowed the gable end of the smaller building to penetrate the building skin and show its roof rakeboards and a doubl-hung window, which provides borrowed light to an adjacent space. Below, there is a space like an inglenook where an antique mantel and raised panel doors and wall treatments suggest more domestically scaled spaces beyond. In another part of the same space, some of the functional but beautiful elements of the former agricultural use remain, attesting to that period in the building's life.

Light provides another part of the warmth and comfort to the space, and almost half of the rear gable end is a two-story combination of fixed and operable glazing, like a giant studio window in an unabashedly modern expression, especially next to the petite openings in the adjoining wings. This year-round residence offers quite a broad range of experiences.

164

*Preceeding pages: The intrusion of the gable end of the adjoining house through the exterior skin provides a visually engaging feature.*

*Facing page: The gable end mezzanine has a floor structure of round logs, positioned edge to edge.*

*The different textures of the wood surfaces are a primary interior design theme.*

*Following pages. One of the gable ends opens to stacked windows with the monolithic glass lights directly let into the timber framing.*

*Left: Antique residential details such as this mantel and paneling complete this niche at the connection to the residential wing.*

*Above: The espalier planting aligns with the wide horizontal siding.*

*The gable-end barn door*
*opening has been substantially*
*enlarged for a two-story*
*monumental window.*

*Views from the balconies
provide different perspectives
of the robust frame.*

# Sheep Hole Farm
## Ottsville, PA

Architect Matt Millan describes his barn clients as passionate and well-informed about their structures and the possibilities available in their new uses. The open-timber barn structures offer opportunities, and the use of systems such as radiant heating, stressed skin panels, artistic lighting, and other concealed infrastructure can make these buildings very livable for families of all sizes. Beginning his career with the New Jersey Barn Company, Matt Millan opened his own office in 1995 with a focus on projects that reinforce the connections between the natural and built environments, incorporating sustainable practices with artful solutions.

For an 82-acre site in Bucks County, Pennsylvania, he started with a site master plan that included the farmhouse, a carriage house, and a bank barn that had been converted into an event space. The owners and architect approached the project with a preservation mind-set to alter the masonry and timber as little as possible while introducing new construction that both related to the agricultural origins of the site and complemented the existing materials. The most striking exterior feature is a new metal corncrib adapted to use as a screened porch overlooking Sheep Hole Creek in the valley.

Inside, the new fireplaces and chimneys are rendered as smooth plastered masses like the traditional lime-washed masonry of the region. The wagon entrance and opposite wall become large glazed openings, serving as the main entrance and a principal source of light, respectively. To supplement the natural light, many other lighting sources are part of an overall scheme that illuminates the whole space to avoid a cavernous feeling. The architect describes the process as similar to lighting a church, providing a balance of up and down lighting, points of emphasis and an overall soft glow.

The bank barn forms the center of a multi-part building, with additions and connecting links joining the carriage house and new volumes to accommodate the supporting program, including the kitchen and guest quarters. This leaves the upper level of the barn unencumbered so the strength of the large timbers and stone walls is fully evident. In this space, the new work is mostly executed in steel to separate it from the historic fabric. The steel assumes multiple forms, from heavy lintels to a light spiral stair, demonstrating a versatility in modern materials that is different from the existing structure.

The site development consisted of new plantings around the main group of buildings to create a precinct separate from the meadows and woodlands. The farm is a year-round retreat for the owners and their children. The original farmhouse now serves as a caretaker's residence.

*Preceding pages*
*Left: The English barn origins are visible in the large central opening, now fully glazed.*

*Right: The steel and concrete are highly finished to complement the more-hand wrought quality of the stone and timber.*

*Right: The sculptured mass of the stuccoed fireplace adds a contrasting textural scale to the rubble stone walls.*

*Facing page: The soaring volume of the interior space is apparent in the cross axis formed by the opposing openings in the stone exterior walls*

# The Sayen Barn Residence
## Villanova, PA

On the rolling meadows that were once part of the estate that formed the setting for the George Cukor film *The Philadelphia Story*, the Sayen Barn possesses the elegance that is a distinguishing feature of the great buildings of Philadelphia's Main Line. Before the railroad and the age of the gentleman's farm, the Welsh and German settlers built stone barns according to their Old World traditions for their livestock, grain and hay. This small barn was modernized in the early twentieth century for the Scott family's prize herd of Ayrshire cattle. Scientific farming methods for dairy production called for the insertion of a new concrete interior structure, but there were few changes on the exterior, save for an ornamental weathervane made for Hope Scott, the inspiration for the heroine of Philip Barry's play turned movie.

When the huge estate began to be subdivided under protective easements from a local land conservancy, the barn and springhouse were not on the preservation list. The present owners, returning from living abroad in the late 1990s, saw the potential in the adaptive re-use of the structure. They worked for over a year with architect John Milner, and sections of the concrete floors were removed to create double-height spaces and cozier areas inside, while little was changed on the exterior so as not to obscure the basic form of the original building. The site contours allowed the garage addition to sit low to one side next to the original earthen ramp to the loft.

Not only did the concrete structure produce obstacles; it also created opportunities in being a neutral backdrop for the new construction, which employs new and salvaged wood for the floors, a central stair and details relating to the domestic architecture of the same era as the original barn structure. The central stair with the flattened balusters is a nod to the original builder's German heritage. The changes in wall thickness related to the earliest form of the building are kept in the smoothly plastered surfaces that contrast with the remaining concrete surfaces.

The owners' desire to respect the original building envelope created challenges for natural light in all of the interior spaces, overcome by introducing interior windows or borrowed lights. This and other challenges were part of the collaborative design and construction process, but it enabled the owners to achieve their goal of a unique residence, not simply a move into "someone else's house." The easements on the whole site have ensured that much of the rural character of the landscape has remained intact just a short distance from the center of Philadelphia.

*Preceding pages: The new interior details play off the masses of the original walls and early twentieth-century concrete structure.*

*Facing page: The detailing of the stair and bridge is an homage to the German family who built the original barn.*

*The limited color palette emphasizes the mass of the building parts in how light and shadow fall across the different surface planes.*

*Following pages: The earthen ramp is a typical feature of the Pennsylvania bank barn.*

# Bellwood Barn

## Saugerties, NY

There is a purity and simplicity about Bellwood Barn that is a tribute to the present owners and the preceding generations. The Dutch barn frame had been dismantled and re-erected as a semi-finished workshop studio. The muscular timber frame had been lovingly restored by experienced framers who respected the original construction when replacing the missing or damaged pieces with new, using traditional methods and joinery, but still showing a difference from the antique members. Dutch barns have a more formal feeling derived from the entrance on the gable end and a greater sense of symmetry than English barns. The redevelopment of the barn from workshop to residence respects this quality.

On a winter weekend in 2011, the present owners saw the property after looking at many weekend home possibilities in the Hudson Valley. After convincing themselves that the project would not be too ambitious, mostly because they intended to avoid big changes, they embarked on the conversion. The new program included three bedrooms, two fully enclosed on a middle level below a master suite separated from the main volume with antique Japanese temple doors acting as movable screens for privacy. The three bathrooms are similarly treated, with the uppermost being open at the top to take in the light from the roof skylights.

The interior design reflects the minimalist aesthetic shared by the owners, and also provides a neutral background for their collection of art and furniture. There is no interior wood to compete with the majesty of the frame. The main floor is polished concrete; the stair and balcony railings are steel pipe. The wall and roof infills are simple white plaster, while the windows are single lights of glass without dividing framework. Simple unadorned light fixtures provide up and down light for direct and indirect illumination. Mezzanines help to create sheltered smaller spaces within the basilica-like volume.

This building clearly shows that new and old can coexist gracefully and play off each other's strengths. The interior is a dialogue between wood and neutral materials. The exterior also introduces new basic geometrical shapes to complement the very basic form of the existing building. The placement and form of the windows is clearly contemporary but not jarring. Without adornment, they fit the building well, as does the simple pent above the main entrance.

The owners feel as if they have created a very personalized space with this minimalist expression. It is a place where the thought and energy put into the design have brought the reward of a relaxing and, in the owners' words, "a zen-inducing space to spend time in."

*The interior and exterior of this building are all about simplicity and functionality.*

*Facing page: New elements are given a completely different treatment from the Dutch barn frame.*

*Right: The transition between inside and outside is very direct—as it always had been.*

*Following pages: The broad gable end of a Dutch barn invites different arrangements for new window openings.*

# Old Stone Farm
## Staatsburg, NY

Situated on 237 acres near Staatsburg, New York, the Old Stone Farm is a spiritual retreat enhanced by the variety of buildings tied together by a common aesthetic intent. The land also plays a significant role in creating the nurturing environment through the relationship of open pastures and wooded areas linked by riding and walking trails to the different building groups. The core of the complex is a Dutch barn and guest house, with new and reconstructed buildings nearby that are the residential heart of the farm. Separate equestrian facilities nearby play a supporting role. Largely unseen in the whole complex are the systems that provide heating, cooling and electricity. The former come from geothermal wells and water storage-facilities underground and in foundation spaces. Solar arrays provide electricity, while hidden generators can provide standby power in the event of a utility loss.

Charles Glasner, an engineer and designer from Highland, New York, has been part of the vision and a prime implementer over the many years the complex has taken shape. Much of the initial work involved the removal of twentieth-century additions to the original buildings on the site and then bringing other old buildings in and re-purposing them. A large English barn became the inn, with ten bedrooms and large interior spaces for gathering. That building was sited on the hillside to reduce the overall mass by burying some of the functions, such as the ground-floor spa, partially into the hillside. The new windows are mostly very small, except for a large opening in the downhill gable facade that lights the main public spaces.

The exterior color palette of "barn red" links the two barns and guest house with some of the smaller outbuildings. The overall fitout of the buildings blurs the boundaries of time through the use of antiques mixed with newer pieces that adhere to an austere Shaker aesthetic, promoting a sense of tranquility and contemplation. Painted furniture and decorations consisting of quilts and woven rugs hung on the walls add color to the interiors.

The English and Dutch barns retain much of their original character inside and out, and that character has been exploited in the new uses for each building. The timber frame of the English barn has multiple scales in the large and small framing members. The guest rooms have been artfully inserted such that the framing in the walls becomes a significant ornamental feature. The hewn unpainted surfaces of the timber play off well against the simple painted paneling and new staircase. The Dutch barn also uses painted and unpainted surfaces to create interest in spaces with little other adornment.

The ease in the way these varied structures coexist is a tribute to the purity of their original aesthetics and the vision of the design team that brought them together. The basic simplicity of the agricultural and residential buildings was a great canvas for the overlays of furnishings and technology, which finally knit things together. They also lay easily on the rustic landscape to create a comforting place for rejuvenation.

Preceding pages: The
furnishings and objects in
this room form a total
environment supported by
the architecture in the
background.

Left: The interior spaces in
the large barn provide
areas for large and small
gatherings.

Below left: An antique
dry sink with the finishes
intact is a reflection on the
passage of time.

Facing page: The large
spaces have a Shaker
simplicity in the old and
new furnishings and
fittings.

Following pages
Left: Traditional
patterned textiles are
functional and decorative
at the same time.

Right: Where there are
small color variations in
the palette, rectilinear and
curved geometries make the
design statement.

The cable-mounted low-voltage lighting offers a different scale and sparkle to the center passage.

Facing page: Agricultural references occur in buildings and objects throughout the site.

Following pages: The site contains large Dutch and English barns with numerous outbuildings and some residential structures.

Facing page: The new
window openings in the
gable end facing the pool
are scaled to relate to the
original door opening.

# Cradle Valley Farm
## New Hope, PA

Some years ago, the stone barn at Cradle Valley Farm became a recording studio for a sound engineer who removed a lot of the original interior framing for his instruments and equipment. The other big changes included the Palladian window at one of the gable ends and a new acoustical treatment to the walls and ceiling. After the barn had lain dormant for several years, the present owners, who were looking for a site with multiple buildings for their own living and musical spaces, bought the property and undertook a restoration of the stone house and a further adaptation of the barn/studio building.

Given the different programmatic goals for the existing and proposed buildings on the site, the owners assembled a collaborative design and construction team consisting of John Milner for the house restoration, local architect Lynn Taylor for the barn, and Curtis Iden as the master builder. The program for the barn consisted of fine-tuning the interior acoustics and environmental systems while also adding back some of the interior features that linked the building to its agricultural past. Only a few of the major timber elements remained, so the builder had to source antique material from other barns in nearby states. These timbers and the new lofts helped soften the acoustics while also paying homage to the original purpose of the building. The ladders and wagon hoist are among the notable historic features re-created.

The new technology is even more understated than the other architectural insertions. The lighting is a combination of low-voltage ambient sources and more specialized fixtures directed at the areas used for music performance. A sophisticated sound system is also largely out of sight since the primary acoustics are a result of the interior finish materials, particularly the wood floor and its

structural framing, over a lower level that acts as a secondary reverberation chamber. The windows required little modification and have a system of shades that help both their thermal and acoustic performance. Similarly, the building envelope and environmental systems required only a few upgrades to maintain the four-season conditioning required for fine musical instruments.

The site has evolved from a working farm to its present domestic state largely because of the architectural quality of the original buildings and the sympathetic site and architectural design. The Palladian window has transformed that facade of the barn to something more like a traditional rustic church from the eighteenth century, while the other facades are closer to their original appearance. With four walls of stone, the barn has a great sense of dignity and permanence, and most of the other masonry openings are unaltered in size. A small eighteenth-century house moved to the site creates the transition zone between the barn and the main house, further domesticating the setting.

The stone bank barns of southeastern Pennsylvania are enduring buildings whose construction, proportions, and utility make them prized parts of the landscape. When one of these buildings can take on a new life that benefits from its intrinsic qualities, in this case great acoustics and a space comfortable for two people or a hundred, it is a tribute to both the original builders and the owner/designer/construction team that respects the history and has the knowledge to exploit it for the new use. This farm group, re-purposed, has benefited greatly from many generations of stewards maintaining the balance of utility, adaptability, and simple beauty. In the words of the Roman architect Vitruvius, "commodity, firmness and delight."

The balconies provide functional space as well as helping with the acoustics in a building re-purposed for musical events as well as smaller gatherings.

*Right:* The wagon hoist is a remnant of the former use.

*Following pages*
*Left:* The Palladian window added by the previous owner changes the whole aspect of the gable end.

*Right:* For the interior, the large window is reminiscent of local colonial churches and meetinghouses.

*The cross bents have elegant joinery supporting the roof purlins.*

The old and new timber elements are almost indistinguishable from each other.

Following pages: The solid stone side walls hardly betray the new interior uses.

# Au Soleil d'Or
## Chester County, PA

The traditional barn form for Chester County in southeastern Pennsylvania is a two-story bank barn with direct access from grade for livestock on the lower level, and grade access to the threshing and storage spaces on the upper level. This type of layout depends on some slope in the land for this bi-level access, so building this type of barn from scratch on a flat site presented a challenge. Using a mature tree as a transitional point, the architects began by gently raising the grade as it approached a traditional earthen ramp to the upper-level entrance. Garden walls also transition to retaining walls in such a way that the artifice seems very natural. The site already contained a traditional farmhouse, extensive gardens, and horse paddocks, so this new structure was part of an overall master plan to unify all of the structures on the property using plantings as a common theme.

The bi-level plan provides stable space below the large open frame space for storage and a play area for the couple's grandchildren. The timber frame came from an old barn and was re-erected on a new stone base story. The stone was carefully chosen to harmonize with the house, and while the basic form of the building is traditional, there are several features that mark it as a newer building. The arched window openings trimmed in brick introduce curves on the facades that continue the themes of the curving garden and ramp walls. The segmental arch that joins the ramp to the barn uses brick masonry for a strong textural and color differentiation from the local stone.

The careful detailing continues to the doors and windows, with their elaborate joinery accented by custom ornamental hardware. The hinges in particular re-create many of the forms found in the eighteenth-century barns and houses in the region. The custom wood-and-metalwork continues into the stable area of the lower level. Timber and stone form the framework for the stall fronts and places for all the tack.

The end result of the multiphase project is a unified group of buildings where special details in the landscape and architectural design tie the ensemble together. The masonry and wood details of the barn bring it a step closer to the main residence by using forms that are not so strictly utilitarian. There is also a touch of whimsy that extends to the weathervane depicting a knight slaying a fire-breathing dragon.

*The upper level is one large
volume, accommodating space
for play as well as its original
role as a hayloft.*

The lower-level stables have individual stalls, a tack room and storage spaces.

Following pages: Landscape walls and plantings help the banked ramp and bridge feel like natural site features.

# Hudson Valley Dutch Barn

## Ulster County, NY

Sometimes two buildings find each other to form a couple. An old stone farmhouse in the Hudson Valley had served as a weekend residence for several years but could not accommodate all of the guests to the 50-acre rural property. The answer was an addition that would complement the historic house but also offer new spatial opportunities and a setting for a collection of Midcentury Modern furniture mixed in with older and newer pieces. An eighteenth-century Dutch barn moved from a site forty miles away and joined to the house by a hyphen structure satisfied the owners' vision.

The house and barn share the elemental prismatic geometry of a gabled box, ornamented by the surface textures of the stone and weathered wood. The Dutch barn form, with an emphasis on the gabled front dominated by a single large opening engages the stone house with its own pattern of small window and door openings on the long facades. The partnership here is very successful and forms the basis for housing an eclectic set of furnishings from many times and places.

The interior volume is dominated by a central "nave" reaching 35 feet at its crown. The side aisles and former lofts provide space for supporting functions on the first floor and bedrooms on the second. Modern insertions like the steel stair and catwalk provide access to the upper-level spaces. Barn structures are particularly conducive to a modern industrial aesthetic that continues the theme of a working building. Natural wood and white plaster illuminated by discrete modern light fixtures are the backdrop for a collection of furniture and textiles. The latter provide much of the color for the space and notes of softness.

The setting is also an important part of the ensemble, with the changing seasons providing additional contrasts in color and outdoor textures. The dry stone site walls, which create delineated precincts near the buildings, are a deconstructed form of the buildings, with a particular resonance with the stone and wood of the house and barn. Other new and old outbuildings on the property also address the rural cycles of work and leisure.

*Facing page: The Dutch barn attached to the house offers large spaces and a mix of traditional and modernist details.*

*Following pages*
*Pages 230–231: Steel post footings are a new detail to create more interior volume and re-level the frame.*

*Page 232: As in many re-purposed Dutch barns, the shoulder space is perfect for bedrooms*

*Page 233: The owners had several antique doors in wood and metal that were used in the space.*

*Pages: 234–35: The furnishings are eclectic, but the combination of new and old construction provides an appropriate setting.*

*Pages 236–37: The barn and house are both simple geometric forms but are very different in character.*

*Facing page: An agricultural tableau in Maine, a house and barn, similar but different.*

# Acknowledgments

I would like to thank Geoffrey Gross and Brandt Bolding for providing images that truly speak for themselves, making my job as author more straightforward. They introduced me to the property owners, designers and constructors whose collective visions made these buildings so distinctive. Their insights struck a number of common chords while also reflecting the diversity of projects represented. I'm also grateful to Rizzoli for another opportunity to work with such a talented team in all aspects of the book design and editing process.

— JAMES B. GARRISON

This book is dedicated to my wife, Catherine Croner, whose awareness and understanding of the exceptional in architecture and design are a great and continued inspiration to me. Thanks to these architects whose barn homes were featured—Kate Johns, AIA, Matthew Millan Architects, Inc., Preston Scott Cohen, Inc., and S. Russell Groves Architect, PC; Constance Kheel, who helped in my search for exceptional barn homes. East Coast Barn Builders for their sensitive restoration on several of the barns, and their work as liaisons. Thanks to Candace Jones and Stephen Phillips, Mr. and Mrs. Mark Waldman, and Mr. and Mrs. Chuck Taylor, who allowed extended stays in their homes while photographic work progressed; Katie Morning, who graciously provided her photographic archive. A special thanks to our editor, Douglas Curran, for his tireless and outstanding work in helping to create this book.

— BRANDT BOLDING

I wish to acknowledge the architects, designers, and builders, who had the vision and know-how to bring these wonderful buildings to life and to express my gratitude for and appreciation of the owners who made them into homes. In particular:

"Hudson Valley Dutch Barn" and "Old Stone Farm" sites designed by Charles Glasner of C. Glasner Design & Associates of Highland, NY. Architectural and interior design/restore/build.

Pool House at Bull Frog Pond, Washington, CT, designed and set up by Karen Davis, ASID of Davis Raines Design.

Au Soleil d'Or, Chester County, PA, by Peter Archer, Archer & Buchanan Architecture, Ltd.

The Sayen Barn Residence, Villanova, PA, John Milner Architects.

Tare Shirt Farm, Peter and Nancy Cook.

Norm and Mary Gronning, Dr. Mead Schafer, Keith Cramer, Steve Swift, "Erhard the timber-framer," Ed Cady, Judith Fleischer, Jordan Schlanger.

Heartfelt thanks go to my co-authors, Jim Garrison, for his insightful text, and Brandt Bolding, for his thoughtful and exquisite photography.

A very special thank-you to all the homeowners, site directors, and caretakers who gave unselfishly of their time and knowledge to accommodate us in the preparation of this book.

I would like to thank, as well, all my good friends at Rizzoli: Doug Curran, editor; Abigail Sturges, book designer; David Morton, associate publisher; Susan Lynch, production manager; and Charles Meirs, publisher; and all the others there who contributed to making this book a reality.

Finally, I dedicate this book to all the timber-framers who continue to carry on in this time-honored tradition.

— GEOFFREY GROSS